DANCER

DANCER

SUZANNE MERRY

PHOTOGRAPHS BY JOHN RUNNING

Charles Scribner's Sons   New York

Text copyright © 1980 Suzanne Merry
Photographs copyright © 1980 John Running

Library of Congress Cataloging in Publication Data

Merry, Suzanne.

Dancer.

1. Jabczenski, Celeste.   2. Dancers—United
States—Biography.   3. Ballet—United States.
I. Running, John.   II. Title.
GV1785.J24M47   792.8′092′4 [B]   79-27379
ISBN 0-684-16440-X

1 3 5 7 9 11 13 15 17 19   MD/C   20 18 16 14 12 10 8 6 4 2

Printed in the United States of America

DANCER

INTRODUCTION

It is not unusual for aspiring young dancers to leave home in order to study with the best teachers in New York or other major cities, but that is only the beginning of their journey: the distance they must travel from the classroom to the stage is perhaps the longest of all. There is so much to learn to become a good performer. I'm proud to say that ten years ago The Joffrey was the first to try to build a bridge between the classroom and the stage by offering young dancers the opportunity to perform and tour with Joffrey II as part of the training process for joining a big company.

This book describes what that journey was like for Celeste Jabczenski, a member of Joffrey II. Celeste had some performing experience already, but when she came to us she was faced with new challenges: making her way in New York and coping with the intense competition and standards of the dance capital of the world; learning to work with choreographers who set a number of new works on the company each year; spending long hours on the road and building stamina; discovering weaknesses and developing strengths under the guidance of the company's directors, Sally Bliss and Maria Grandy; and always refining her technique. As a young professional with Joffrey II, she looks forward to the day when she may be chosen for our main company.

This is the story of one young dancer, but it is not unlike that of many other young people who want so very much to dance.

Robert Joffrey

Celeste Jabczenski is a dancer with the junior company of the Joffrey Ballet in New York City, known as Joffrey II. Like most ballet dancers in a similar position at her age (Celeste is eighteen), she has traveled a long road to professional status in the dance capital of the world, garnering intense formal training and much performing experience along the way.

A dancer's schedule is not an easy one, and Celeste's is no exception. Five or six days a week she travels on the subway to New York's midtown City Center Dance Theater for company class in the morning, followed by rehearsal until five-thirty or six o'clock. When the company is touring, which they do several times yearly, logging hundreds of miles, there are hours spent on the bus, last-minute rehearsals and warm-ups, evening performances, and postperformance receptions and dinners. In bed by midnight or two o'clock in the morning, the dancers must be up early the next morning and back

on the bus to travel for six hours or so to the next one-night stand.

For Celeste, with her sights set on joining the Joffrey's major company within the next year, the grueling schedule demands concentration, dedication, and sacrifice. The aspiring dancer has little time for a social life or even for schooling, few opportunities for meeting anyone outside the tightly knit community of the ballet company, and even less time for just relaxing.

But dancing can be a glorious experience; present rewards are great, and hope for the fulfillment of a promising career even greater. Celeste is a strong and often dazzling dancer, possessed of seemingly effortless extension, graceful carriage, the gift of speed, and exquisite control. Remarkably enough for her age—and having taken up ballet seriously rather later than most dancers—she has already danced with two professional companies and has every opportunity for an exciting future. She is clearly on her way up.

Celeste started taking ballet classes once a week at the age of ten with her mother, Rosemary Jabczenski, Alan McCarter, and Kelly Brown at the Phoenix School of Ballet to improve her performance in gymnastic competition. At that time gymnastics was her main interest; she had even thought about training for the Olympics, and ballet was merely a sideline. By the age of twelve, however, she had given up gymnastics and had earnestly begun her ballet training with classes every day.

When she was fifteen she left home for the first time to attend a four-week summer program at the Atlanta Ballet on scholarship, having declined a similar offer from Ballet West in Salt Lake City. As it turned out she stayed on in Atlanta for two and a half years, from January 1976 to April 1978. She became a member of the Atlanta Ballet's corps de ballet of thirty-six dancers, dancing in such ballets as *The Nutcracker, Swan Lake, Les Sylphides, Giselle,* and *Serenade.* In the meantime, she attended high school for a year and a half.

Since dancing was consuming more and more of her time, she finally finished high school by correspondence.

Atlanta became "a home away from home" for Celeste. She loved the city and felt comfortable there, living with two families before finding her own apartment. Robert Barnett, the director of the company, was "like a father to me," she says; "he was really special." Though the rest of the company and the administration wanted her to stay on indefinitely, to join a newly formed touring company made up of members of the parent ballet company, Mr. Barnett urged her, when the opportunity arose, to leave Atlanta to try her luck in New York. He knew, as she did intuitively, that she would never fulfill her potential as a professional dancer until she joined a major New York company.

That opportunity presented itself in the spring of 1978, when Celeste was seventeen. Robert Joffrey, director of New York's Joffrey Ballet, saw her dance at the Southeastern Regional Ballet Festival, where he was a master teacher, and was interested. He offered her a scholarship to the American Ballet Center, the company school for the Joffrey Ballet, and an invitation to join Joffrey II as soon as there was an opening.

At the same time, Celeste had received another offer from a New York school. Jacques d'Amboise had come to Atlanta to perform with "Stars of the American Ballet," and while there auditioned Celeste in a private class on the recommendation of Mr. Barnett. He immediately offered her a scholarship to the School of American Ballet, George Balanchine's school for the New York City Ballet. The offer was exciting, but Celeste found the Balanchine style foreign to her own ballet training; in addition, the Joffrey offer presented the more immediate prospect of performing with Joffrey II as well as studying. Recalling it as "a decision I had to make on my own" and a matter of "good timing," Celeste left Atlanta for New York City.

The first days in New York were both trying and exciting. She arrived on June 24, 1978, with seven suitcases, minimal money, and two weeks to kill before the beginning of the Joffrey scholarship program. She stayed at the Katharine House, a residence for women on Thirteenth Street in Greenwich Village. Her room, as she remembers, "was the

size of a closet. I could stretch out my arms lying in bed and touch both walls; there wasn't even enough room for my suitcases!" Still, it was a nice enough room, with a pleasant fifth-floor view. "It was good to have some place to come back to where I could be alone after battling the crowds in the streets and in ballet classes" — even though the communal bathroom, pay phones on every other floor, and cafeteria-style dining room took some getting used to, especially the cafeteria-style food.

That first week she recorded in her journal: "I've been making friends a little more day by day, but not any good friends. So I play cards by myself and just do things to pass the

time until I can find a good friend to be with and do things with. This whole week I've been kind of lonely and homesick here. It would be good to have someone to talk to."

But within a few days she had made a few friends, explored the neighborhood, received a class schedule for the David Howard School of Ballet, and learned how to get there by subway.

In the airy, spacious studios of the David Howard School, Celeste took two or three classes a day for two weeks prior to beginning the Joffrey program. She took technique, *pas de deux,**and *pointe* classes. In class and around the studio she saw many well-known professional dancers, among them Starr Danias, Burton Taylor, Leslie Browne, Gelsey Kirkland,

* See the glossary on page 61 for definition of this and other dance terms.

and others from the American Ballet Theatre, the New York City Ballet, and The Joffrey.

"I liked being in David Howard's classes because I was exposed to so many good dancers. They had their own personal styles, and I was trying to work on a style for myself. Coming to New York and dancing for a couple of weeks helped me be a bit more relaxed when I went to Joffrey.

"Every day I felt a little more accustomed to the atmosphere and to David Howard's style of teaching. The first day I was really nervous and uptight, and I felt different from everyone else. But every day after that I felt a little more in tune with things and a little more open and ready to dance and ready to push myself. It was good for me.

"At first I was really sore and my neck was swollen from doing *port de bras* — which David Howard gives a lot of. I love his classes. Technically, they're fairly easy, but he gives great combinations. He gives a slow *barre* where you can get warmed up, but things really move in the center. He does stretches with the leg on the barre, and in the center you lie on the floor and do stretches with your legs, which I love. Then he gives *adagio* in the center; you put your pointe shoes on and he does a couple of *pirouette* combinations and then jump combinations and something across the floor, and class is over. It goes quickly, but it's very tiring."

Despite the progress she was making and her obvious enjoyment of ballet classes and all the other new experiences, Celeste was still plagued by homesickness and a need to bolster her spirits with the promise of soon being able to join a company. "You don't realize how much you have at your own house, in your own state, or in your ballet company until you leave home and go to a bigger city like New York. I never really knew what competition was until I came here. And you never realize how much you appreciate your home, your parents, your family until you're on your own and far from home, especially in a place like New York where everything is fast and grubby and competitive. It's a real rat race! But I loved New York. I knew if I could just get in there and fight, everything would be all right.

"You have to aim for something important when you really want to make it here because the competition is so rough.

Nobody ever said it was going to be easy here, but I feel that's what the competition is all about. And I feel good as an individual if I can just tell myself 'don't be afraid, stand out, step out, show what you have.' It's always one more step up the ladder. I kept reminding myself then that it had just been one week, and who knew what could develop in six weeks!"

After two weeks at the David Howard School, Celeste began the scholarship at The Joffrey, taking classes with Meredith Baylis, formerly with the Ballet Russe de Monte Carlo, Basil Thompson, a former soloist with the American Ballet Theatre and ballet master at The Joffrey, and a guest teacher from Russia, Nikolai Zhukovin. As a scholarship student she was required to take two technique classes and a pointe class daily, in addition to classes in character dancing and pas de deux. Classes were crowded — in her first one, there were more than a hundred students — but she was quickly noticed. On the second day she was asked by Miss Baylis to join a smaller and more advanced class.

"I couldn't believe she noticed me out of 120 people. It was so crowded that we had to do everything in two groups and the class was nearly three hours long. We were all kicking one another every time we did *tendus* at the barre; it was pretty comic. I would just work through the crowds and get up in front for the center combinations. I was usually in the front line in every class, which was a good break."

The classes were fun, though not as challenging as Celeste had hoped. "That first week they were very basic, so all of us could get adjusted. In Miss Baylis's pointe class we did échappés and passés and a few turns—but nothing as difficult as I'd expected. I thought I needed harder stuff, especially more center work. Nikolai Zhukovin didn't speak English, so he had to demonstrate every combination and he gave very basic things, too—slow, strengthening exercises like repeated relevés with one leg on the barre. But he always gave hard adagios at the barre that no one could seem to do. I loved his classes because they were such a variation from Miss Baylis's and Mr. Thompson's."

After the first two weeks at the Joffrey school, Celeste began to wonder when her chance would come to join Joffrey II, or indeed whether anyone at the company knew that she was even at the school. However, she was soon invited to take the company class, and was then asked to join Joffrey II.

Celeste started out understudying members of the first company in such ballets as Frederick Ashton's *A Wedding Bouquet*, Kurt Jooss's *The Green Table*, Agnes de Mille's *Rodeo*, and *New York Export, Opus Jazz* by Jerome Robbins.

Joffrey II was formed in 1969 for the purpose of training soloists for the first company. The dancers are treated as bona-fide professionals, learning all aspects of staging and performing, and earning a stipend year-round and a full salary while on tour. The company has twelve performing members and four understudies, and is under the artistic direction of Sally Bliss and her associate, Maria Grandy, both former dancers with the Joffrey Ballet. Both teach classes (with occasional guest teachers such as Donald Mahler, David Howard, Robert Barnett, and Marjorie Mussman) and run rehearsals, in addition to finding new ballets and choreographers for the company, organizing tours, and taking a personal interest in each of their young dancers. Celeste recalls that after her first

couple of classes she was invited to Sally's office to work privately on a problem: a tendency toward hyperextension in her legs, which resulted in incorrect placement of her hip.

"She told me she wanted me to really get in there and learn, especially in class when she doesn't have time to help me privately. She gets across something of the inner feeling of dancing, in a way other teachers can't. She has told me, 'Celeste, you've got to feel it in your soul…'"

Maria, in Celeste's words, is "gung-ho on everything" and very energetic. Extremely meticulous, she has the job of finishing and polishing each of the ballets that the company performs, urging the dancers to work harder to extend themselves.

A typical day for Celeste and the other members of Joffrey II starts with class at the City Center rehearsal studio on Fifty-fifth Street at ten in the morning, followed by rehearsal until five or six o'clock. Usually, she says, "I jump out of bed at about eight—I'm so fast in the morning. I make some hot chocolate and sometimes I eat a bran muffin. Then I get dressed and catch the subway at about nine o'clock. I get to City Center by nine-twenty, change, and start stretching. I'm usually the first one there."

The other dancers start spilling into the classroom at about nine-thirty, stretching at the barres and on the floor to warm up. An old upright piano is in one corner of the sixth-floor studio, and dance bags — large shoulder bags stuffed with dance clothes, shoes, and other essentials—are propped in the corners and beneath the bench against one wall.

As with every ballet class, this one begins with barre work in the usual order, starting with *pliés* to stretch the Achilles tendon and warm up the muscles of the calves and thighs—usually two *demi-pliés* and a *grand plié* in each position, followed by a port de bras. Next are the tendus and *dégagées*, extending the foot to point front, side, and back and returning

it to *sur le cou de pied*, the tendus brushing the floor, the dégagées held a few inches off the ground. Following are the *ronds de jambes*, the circle of the leg that enforces a controlled *turnout, par terre* and *en l'air*, separated by quick *frappés* and *petits battements* or *battements serrés*. Sally or Maria explains and usually demonstrates each exercise in full, stopping class occasionally for personal corrections or sympathetic comments. The dancers are warned against being too academic and careful, but admonished to be precise. After a

stretch, the barre finishes with grand battements, the big kicks usually done in sets of eight to each direction. At the barre Celeste concentrates particularly hard on working her feet, her extension, and her placement.

With perspiration beading on their foreheads, students shed warm-up layers of dancewear as the barre goes on. Like most dancers, Celeste doesn't feel thoroughly warmed up and ready to dance until she's broken a first sweat. Rather than wearing many layers of warm-up clothes, she prefers to get warmed up by simply working hard at the barre. She usually starts to sweat and feel flexible by the time class has progressed to tendus.

Moving to the center, the class is usually given a multiple pirouette combination, an adagio (the slow, control-testing combination, often incorporating *développés*, *promenades*, and relevés on pointe or demi-pointe—Celeste's least favorite part of class), one or two small, quick jump combinations with beats to warm up the feet, and, to end, several big, traveling combinations across the floor from corner to corner that develop *ballon*, speed, and musicality.

On a normal day class is given from ten o'clock to twelve, from ten to eleven-thirty if the company is on a tight schedule. At noon the dancers are given a twenty-minute break. They order out for soda or iced coffee; the girls put on their pointe shoes to warm up. Celeste goes over ballets in her head, reviewing and talking about the sections of the ballets to be rehearsed with her partners.

If a new choreographer is about to "set a ballet on the

company"—that is, create a new work—he or she will often
watch class first before working with the dancers in rehearsal;
otherwise Maria or Sally directs the ballets being rehearsed.
Rehearsal lasts until two o'clock, some of the dancers working
with the choreographer or ballet mistress, others learning ballets at the side of the room or in an empty studio downstairs.
From two o'clock to three everyone takes a lunch break, coming back to rehearse for the rest of the afternoon.

"I hate the afternoons after break. All morning you're just
dying to get to your break at two o'clock; but an hour is just
enough time to run and get something to eat and run back.
And when I come back I'm usually really cold; there's never
enough time to warm up since we have to start right away. So
I'm always stiff for the rest of the afternoon."

Rehearsals can sometimes be tedious, seeming to drag on for hours, especially if one isn't in the ballet being rehearsed. But when a new ballet is being set on the company or if the company is about to go on tour, the pace becomes more hectic, the dancers scrambling to learn new parts or understudy others, and putting the finishing touches on pieces already in the repertory before going out on the road.

After rehearsal Celeste heads back to the subway, at the peak of rush hour, and home—usually an hour-long ride.

Unless the company is performing in New York, her evenings and weekends are her own — time to relax, to take in an occasional movie or dinner with friends, or to shop. Most of her free time, however, is spent doing her laundry, writing letters, and sewing pointe shoes—a constant task.

"I wear Capezio's Contempora pointe shoes; I order mine with a three-quarter shank and a half-size longer vamp. It's like ordering a shoe made to my own requirements, and I think my feet look good in them. But they don't last very long

—two weeks at the most—and they're awfully expensive. Fortunately when you get into a company they buy all your shoes for you. Most people use some type of padding inside their pointe shoes, like moleskin or lamb's wool, but it feels better to me without any padding inside so I can feel my feet.

"My ballet shoes last about two months. It's hard to break them in when they're new because they're so stiff, so I put some hot water or a shoe stretch in them and then they fit like a glove."

Like most dancers, Celeste watches her diet very carefully. She usually keeps her weight down to about 102 or 103 pounds, though it's not much of a problem since she dances all week and has little time to eat. "Once in a while I go off my diet a little and eat ice cream and candy bars for instant energy, but afterward I feel guilty. I always have a harder time disciplining myself on the weekends, when I'm not dancing. It's a big sacrifice to make yourself not eat and stay thin, but you have to live with yourself if you don't."

If Celeste is disciplined it's because, like all good dancers, she works at it. No matter how much joy one can derive from dancing, sometimes the constant drudgery of work can be tiresome, and a dancer has to push herself constantly to get to the top, forgetting the aches and pains and prodding her body to work harder.

"Sometimes I've had to remind myself that this is my life; other people go to work every morning to do their jobs, and I've got to go to my class every morning. I've got to make the

best of every class. I feel that I'm well disciplined: I don't smoke, I don't drink; I'm always early for class and rehearsal; I try to be dependable."

Being a successful dancer also demands something of a sacrifice in the way of the personal and social life that most young people enjoy. Besides the necessity of a curtailed education and the financial burden that ballet training imposes on a young dancer's family, it also requires a measure of determined independence on the part of the dancer. Ballet students generally have to make a decision about their career in their early teens, and often must strike out on their own and move to a major city where professional ballet schools are found. Celeste is not unique among dancers in having left home at a very early age — in her case, at fifteen, to go to Atlanta and then on to New York. Though she tries to make herself feel at home in her surroundings, she often misses her real home and family, and flies back to Arizona to visit whenever she has the chance.

At this point in her life she doesn't have any special boyfriend or boyfriends, and feels that it's sometimes hard to meet people in the big city, particularly since the only people with whom she has frequent contact are her fellow dancers in Joffrey II. However, she doesn't feel that she is missing anything; dancing is fulfilling and time-consuming enough, in her opinion, and the prospects that it offers for the future more than make up for any other possibilities ignored or put aside.

Of course the most exciting aspect of her career right now is the opportunity to perform, which occurs most often when Joffrey II is on tour. The company makes two to three tours yearly, a series of six to eight weeks of single-night performances in cities and towns of all different sizes across the country. Because of its size, Joffrey II is able to perform in varied and out-of-the-way places where the larger, major Joffrey company cannot afford to go.

On one tour of the West and Midwest, Celeste's younger sister Liz came to Denver to audition with the company and was awarded a scholarship to the American Ballet Center. She now shares an apartment in New York with Celeste. Another tour took the company through the Deep South and lasted six weeks, ending with several performances in New England and upstate New York. Like previous tours, it was a series of one-night stands, broken up by long bus rides from city to city, and state to state, that left the dancers barely enough time to rehearse, dress, and warm up before the curtain rose. After the performances there were parties and receptions; company members would get back to their hotel around midnight, grab a bite to eat, and collapse into bed for a few hours sleep before it was time to leave again at seven or eight o'clock the next morning. There are usually only a few days off in the course of these six-week tours; a typical one might be spent in a twelve-hour bus ride. If the entourage arrives early enough the

dancers get out to do a little sightseeing or, if the hotel is near a theater, to see a movie.

Sally and Maria take turns going with the company on tours, smoothing the details of performance, and trying to maintain a sense of discipline in the ranks of the dancers— which isn't always easy. Antics on one tour included the company's meeting up with a slew of Coast Guard men at one hotel, who asked Celeste out for a "nightcap" after the performance (an invitation which she declined), and then splashed her name all over the company tour bus with red paint; and losing at the beach a bedspread they had spirited out of Celeste's hotel room.

"It seemed I was blamed for everything on that tour," Celeste sighs. After the Coast Guard incident, "I was the criminal. Every time something like this happened they would nod at me and say, 'You again!'"

About the tour of the Southern states, Celeste remembers: "It was very hard; I didn't think it would be so tiring. I think everyone started to get run-down really fast the first week because the strain was such a shock. Another girl and I got stomach flu, so the company was dancing with four girls instead of six, which made things difficult. The performances went very well, but all the girls were dancing four ballets a night. I felt really bad about letting them down, but there was nothing I could do about it. I was lying in the wings moaning, feeling achy and terrible until someone from the audience came backstage to drive me home. And another boy started to get sick in the wings during a performance, just as he was about to go on stage. A doctor had to drive him home to the hotel."

The cities rolled by so fast that the dancers often forgot where they had been from night to night. "We would be in Georgia one night, then Mississippi the next, and so on, until we couldn't remember what state we were in."

On the whole, however, it was a good tour and a great experience for Celeste. The performances were exciting, the audiences were enthusiastic, and the members of Joffrey II learned to rely on each other. "It was nice on tour because everyone in the company got really close to everyone else. We

are anyway, but everybody knew it was a hard tour, so we helped each other out.

"When we were on tour Sally had a little conference with each of us on the bus one day. She told me that she wanted me to stay in Joffrey II another year. That's okay with me; I need to be here. I haven't been with the company very long in comparison to some of the others, so I want to stay here longer before moving up. I need to learn a lot more about performing and dealing with tough situations, like touring.

"When I first joined the company there was a girl here who was just about to get into Joffrey I. She had been the principal dancer with Joffrey II, and she had been doing everything, dancing in almost every ballet. And I remember that when she did join the first company she was very depressed because she would dance in maybe one ballet, ten minutes a night. It's really a radical change. Before then I never thought about it. I assumed getting into Joffrey I would be more of what I was accustomed to, just being paid more and getting more recognition. It's not that way at all.

"And another thing Sally said to me was, 'When you go into the first company, we want you to be the *best* you can be!' I said all right, I'll try. I mean, I want to go in doing better parts instead of just standing on the side, doing occasional roles. So I don't mind the wait. I need the strength. I'm also still very young in comparison to a lot of other people when they get their start as professionals.

"Sally also told me I have to listen to my music more. She ordered me to go home and put classical music on my tape recorder and study the phrasing as I listened—and turn on disco music later! She also said they were pleased with my progress overall: I don't have any special problems to worry about or any bad habits, except the music that I have to work on, and harder work in general. But that's the reason I'm here."

Looking ahead to the possibility of dancing with the Joffrey Ballet, in addition to the thrill of top billing and exposure to

some of the finest ballet dancers in the country, Celeste antici-
pates a different kind of touring and performing schedule.
"Joffrey does tour to major cities like Chicago and San Fran-
cisco. They've been to Mexico and Russia and have danced in
European cities like London and Vienna. No one-night stands
or spending all day on the bus; it's against the dancers' union
regulations. Joffrey II isn't union, but that's all right. It's all
part of the experience we need." In addition, the first company presents lengthy yearly seasons in New York, something
Joffrey II is unable to do.

During vacations and breaks between performing seasons
and the rigors of a daily rehearsal schedule, Celeste is often at
a loss for ways to keep busy. "The first time I had six days off
in the city, I didn't know what to do with myself. I missed
dancing! I was really excited to get back to work. You know,
sometimes you get to the point where you say to yourself, 'Oh
no, another day of work, all day....' I started getting like that
before we left on tour, because we were doing the same things
all day; I always knew the schedule in advance. But being
away from it, even for just six days, I really missed it. I mean,
it's the only thing I would ever do. I don't know what I'd do if
I couldn't dance."

Celeste can't envision going to college or working at a nine-
to-five job. There is always the possibility of teaching ballet
classes, but she is not enthusiastic about it. "Once I taught
class for my Mom. I made the barre an hour before I realized
there were only twenty minutes left for the center. I feel shy
about teaching. I'd never be able to yell at students.... My

family has said I should go into modeling if I ever quit dancing, but I'm really not interested in it. Sometimes my grandmother calls after rehearsal when I'm so tired, and she'll say, 'Do you really like dancing? You're killing yourself. Do you really like all this work?' And I'll say, 'Grandma, of course. That's why I'm in it.'"

Once Celeste was spotted by a film casting director in a New York supermarket and asked if she'd be interested in a movie part, but she was hesitant about it. "I wouldn't mind being in the movies, but I'd want to dance at the same time. I'd never quit dancing for it."

Since joining Joffrey II, she has had a lot of performing experience, on several tours and in New York at Lincoln Center's Avery Fisher Hall, and at the New York State Theater with the first company and guest star Rudolf Nureyev. "I don't work very well unless I perform. It seems like a whole other level to me, performing, than taking class every day. When I first came to New York and I was just taking classes, I thought, it's going to be so long before I get into Joffrey II and start performing. But then it went so fast. It was incredible. And I thought, I don't know how people can just take class day in and day out without performing, because it's such an essential part of dance. You need it. Whenever we did have a day off on tour I felt uneasy, as if I really should have been doing something that evening.

"When I go to David Howard's class on my day off, I see the same people there all the time. All they do is take class. I don't know how they do it. I guess it's good for you if you just want to build up a lot of technique, but then it's like going to a gym and working out every day but never playing, or going to college and never doing anything with your education. It's nice to have that kind of time once in a while. Every now and then they'll give us a period of maybe two weeks to study at the Joffrey school without rehearsals. But I think that's all I could take.

"I enjoy having my one class or perhaps two classes a day, but I enjoy rehearsing more because I can come out of myself. In class I feel so restrained; you have to do what everyone else is doing. When you do a piece in rehearsal and especially in performance, everyone has basically the same steps to do. But when *you* do it, you can kind of come out of yourself and put your own little touch into it—whereas in class you can't do that much because you're working basically for technique."

The principle behind a ballet class, of course, is that this is where the building blocks of technique and style are formed —blocks that come together only in the continuity provided by a single piece of choreography. Class itself, made up of a number of short combinations at the barre and in the center, is not always gratifying because it does not require the sustained effort and energy of a performance, in which one has something to do from the beginning to the end—even if it only consists of standing still onstage or rushing on and off through the wings. Performance requires one burst of concentration and energy from start to finish.

"I feel much more competitive, too, in rehearsal or performance, especially when I'm dancing in a piece with five other people. In class, I know a lot of people are watching me and in a way there is some competition there. But I really enjoy it when, for instance, Maria and Sally will say 'Okay, let's run this ballet and the rest of you sit down and watch.' Since we're so close and we spend so much time together, you can say to yourself, 'Oh, my peers are watching.' You can kind of show off, and that's fun once in a while. And it's nice when other dancers get up at the end and say, 'You know, that arm was wrong. It would look better if you did it this way.' Everybody in our company wants to make everybody else look good.

"And they do give us leeway in a lot of the ballets to do our own things, especially in Brett Raphael's *Suite Paganini*, and in *Continuo*. That's one thing I like about the company — giving us that freedom to create a character in the role that we're doing. Even if it's not a major role, we can put ourselves into it."

Among Celeste's favorite roles are Frederick Ashton's *Monotones II*, which she learned as part of The Joffrey's policy of training Joffrey II dancers in the main company's repertory, and Choo San Goh's *Momentum;* they are also the two ballets in which she's most prone to stage fright. *Monotones*, characterized by the clean and elegant restraint of Ashton's classicism, is particularly challenging. In it, a girl and two boys, clad in stark white unitards—leotards and tights in one suit— mark out diagonal lines on stage, gently turning, supporting, and manipulating each other through cool poses.

"I really get nervous about *Monotones* because the music is so slow and all the movement is so visible. For instance, there's one part where we just step into fifth position and lift one foot into *passé* and bend to the side. And you can't waver or shake

at all. I get so nervous for those parts because I want to make everything so neat and clean. But most of the ballets we do in Joffrey II are fairly calm, and you can kind of cover up—like Ichinoke's *Kami no Yama,* a Japanese dance, or *Suite Paganini.* There are some tricky things, like a lot of hops on pointe in some of them, but otherwise they're fairly easy. In *Continuo* you can't cover up mistakes so well. I'm not really a lyrical dancer at all. I'm more of a sharp dancer, and *Continuo* is very lyrical. The music is soft, and I just don't move well softly. That's one of the problems I have to work on.

"Aside from these, I like Daryl Gray's *Threads from a String of Swing,* a jazzy forties' piece. It's really a gut buster. When we were on tour, a lot of older people would ask if I really enjoyed doing it. Yes! Since I didn't grow up in the forties it's a challenge to me to represent the forties the best I can. At receptions people would say, 'That's exactly what we did, exactly what we wore; that could have been us up there.' And you know, it felt good to hear that people felt that way."

Looking ahead to the future of her career, Celeste is eager to tackle all of the Joffrey I repertory, which is very diverse, ranging from contemporary ballets to those more than a century old. She is especially interested in modern, dramatic ballets, though she doesn't think she's ready for such roles now. "For instance, we have Ron Cunningham's ballet called *Incident at Blackbriar* in the Joffrey II repertory. It's between two girls, and it's really a deep, dramatic ballet. I'd like to work into it, but I can't see myself doing it now." She also realizes that the very dramatic ballets often require an older, more mature dancer who can call on a lifetime of experience to help her summon the emotional depth necessary to portray such tragic or moving characters as Giselle or Juliet.

"But I think I'd like to do a couple of classics, too, like *Romeo and Juliet, Don Quixote, Giselle,* or *Swan Lake.* But the only *Romeo and Juliet* the Joffrey does is a modern one by Oscar Araiz. It's very different, but I like it. You don't expect to see that kind of movement with the familiar Prokofiev music. I think one of the reasons I always enjoy it is because the music is so beautiful.

"I love the dancing in *Don Q.* I feel that's the type of dancer I am. It's more suited to me than *Romeo and Juliet.* And I love all the Balanchine ballets. I'm not a very good jumper, so I don't like to jump fast, but I like very abstract movement, very clean and precise and sharp. The Balanchine style has a sharpness to it that the romantic and lyrical ballets don't have at all. I'm better at the sharp kinds of things. I'm more of a brisk dancer than a lyrical one. I feel more secure in stronger parts. I love to just battement my leg up high; it's exciting. And I love working with a partner. It really gives you an uplift! I also have a good time just talking with my partners while we're dancing and rehearsing. They make me feel very secure in a part."

Currently Celeste's partners include Joffrey II members Luis Perez, Glenn Edgerton, and Tom Mossbrucker. "I dance with Luis a lot; he's my partner in *Momentum.* Our height is

very compatible and we look similar, with dark hair and dark eyes. We work very well together. I dance with Tom in *Threads*, and Glenn is one of my best friends."

Among the dancers in the first company, Celeste would like to dance with Dennis Poole ("Since he helped us with *Monotones* I got to know him better, and he partnered me a lot in rehearsals helping me learn it."), Gregory Huffman, and Burton Taylor. And of course she'd "jump at the chance" to dance with Mikhail Baryshnikov.

Working with Joffrey II and learning to live on her own in New York has been a rich and maturing experience for Celeste, but she has a long way to go. "I feel like a professional, but I have a lot to learn. I always try to demand the same kind of meticulousness of myself that my mother demands.

"Right now I don't have any dancers that I consider idols or that I consciously try to model myself after. I love Patricia McBride, and Gelsey Kirkland is just incredible. And there are quite a few ballerinas in Joffrey I that I just love, but I try to grasp things from everyone I'm around, whether they're in Joffrey II or Joffrey I, to see if there are good points that I can apply to myself.

"But lately I haven't thought about any particular person to strive to be like. I just want to strive to be the very best I can be, and be myself, and if I'm lucky maybe someday someone will say, 'Oh, I'd like to be like her.'"

GLOSSARY

adagio: a series of sustained and perfectly controlled dance movements, displaying balance, grace, and line

ballon: lightness and elasticity in jumping

barre: the wooden rail a dancer uses for support while exercising

battement: extension of the leg

> **grand battement:** extension and brush of the leg to hip level or higher
>
> **petit battement:** a beating of the foot from front to back on the ankle of the supporting leg, turned out
>
> **battement serré:** a fast tapping of the toe of the working leg on the instep of the standing foot, usually on a *relevé*

dégagée: low extension and brush of the leg with toe pointed

développé: a gradual unfolding of the leg toward the front, side, or back

échappé: opening of the leg from a closed position to *relevé* or *sauté*

en l'air: in the air; off the floor or ground

frappé: a striking of the toe of the working leg against the floor from the ankle to front, side, and back

par terre: on the floor or ground (as opposed to *en l'air*)

pas de deux: a dance by two persons

passé: a movement in which one leg passes behind or in front of the other, the toe brushing the knee of the standing leg

pirouette: a turn on one foot or on *pointe*

plié: a bending of the knees to the side, with the back held straight

    demi-plié: a slight bending of the knees with the heels on the ground

    grand-plié: a full bending of the knees with the heels off the ground

pointe: the tip of the toe; a position on the extreme tips of the toes

port de bras: an exercise for developing the technique of moving the arms properly

positions of the feet, the five basic: FIRST POSITION: heels together, toes turned out; SECOND POSITION: feet in a parallel line, separated by a distance of about twelve inches and both turned outward; THIRD POSITION: the heel of one foot resting against the instep of the other; FOURTH POSITION: one foot resting about twelve inches in advance of the other, both turned out, weight center; FIFTH POSITION: feet turned out and pressed closely together, the heel of one against the toe of the other

promenade: a turning on the supporting leg with the working leg extended, lifting the heel slightly as turn is made on supporting leg; can also be done on *pointe*, being turned by a partner

relevé: a rising up onto full *pointe* or half *pointe* from the flat of the feet

rond de jambe (par terre): a circular movement of the leg, with working leg extended to front, continuing to side and back, toe on floor, ending in first position with both feet on the floor

sauté: jump

sur le cou de pied: a position in which the working foot is placed above the ankle of the standing leg, either on *relevé* or flat

tendu: a movement in which the leg is extended to the front, toe on floor, and then returned to the fifth position, weight center; can be repeated to the side and to the back

turnout: the turning out of the legs from the hips, with the feet back to back or heel to heel